LETTERS TO THE BLACK COMMUNITY

Dr. Eugena K. Griffin

Creating Change Publishing, LLC
Brooklyn, New York

This publication contains the opinion and ideas by its author. The solutions outlined in this book may not be suitable for every individual. No warranty is made with respect to the accuracy of the results postulated. Thus, the author and publisher specifically disclaim any responsibility for any liability, loss, or risk (financial, personal, or otherwise) which may be claimed or incurred as a consequence, directly or indirectly, of the use and application of any of the contents of this book.

Published by Creating Change Publishing, LLC
P.O. Box 80327
Brooklyn, New York 11208

Manufactured in the United States of America

ISBN: 978-0-9851607-0-8

ATTENTION: Universities, Colleges, other Institutions of Multicultural, Black, and/or Diversity Studies
This book is available at large quantity discounts with bulk purchase for educational use. For more information, contact Creating Change Publishing, LLC, P.O. Box 80327, Brooklyn NY 11208 or 718-802-8965. Please provide quantity needed and a description of how the book will be used.

Table of Contents

Acknowledgements

This book has been edited by a team of brilliant and talented individuals, whom worked with me to aid in making my first book project its best.

Ms. Karen Clements
Dr. Kenia Johnson

Thanks to my editors, I was able to put on paper what my Creator laid on my heart to Educate, Encourage, & Empower the community.

To my best friend of 21 yrs & counting, Mrs. Adrianne C. Monroe, thanks for your tireless effort in photography and book cover design.

Special Thanks to my Spiritual Leaders

Rev. David Keith Brawley
Rev. Lesley Shannon
Rev. Johnny Ray Youngblood

Thank you for being obedient to our Creator as He gives you instruction on how to instill the importance of a community orientation within our people, and guides you as you provide immeasurable spiritual knowledge.

Foreword

The intent of this book is to raise awareness within the Black community. The focus is on the maladaptive influence of the systemic structures of racism; specifically, the resulting symptoms of an illness which plagues the Black community, internalized oppression. I present a multitude of ways our illness lends to the corruption of our psyche and communal energies. This book is a compilation of messages delivered at community speaking engagements and extensive thoughts formed during exploration on the subject matter as a student and developing career professional.

The book is divided into four sections with letters directed to important groups within the Black community: The Collective, Black Men, Black Women, and Black Youth. In each section, the letters address the symptomatic manifestation of internalized oppression within each group and offers remedies targeted specifically to them.

This book is relevant for all readers interested in thoughtful exploration of the maladaptive behaviors displayed within Black communities that hinder growth, communal energies, and healing from generational racial oppression. It is my hope that we will become more conscious of our actions, spoken words, resume our communal spirit, and make positive changes where necessary.

Meditate, absorb, and allow the words to assist in your process of change…

Introduction

Racism Today, 21st Century Manifestation

Do you believe racism does not exist? How does racism manifest itself today? Some of us buy into the illusion that it is obsolete because we have lived to see the first Black president. On the other hand, a few of us are unaware of its appearance because we have yet to experience a blatant act of racial discrimination. Additionally, we confuse the definition of racism and often minimize it to prejudice; assumptions or stereotypes about the abilities, motives, and intentions of others based on race. Racism is a system consisting of hidden and known policies, practices, and laws used to keep a group of people at a disadvantage compared to the majority class. In America's history, Whites developed racist tools, institutions and policies to keep Blacks from advancing.

Racism is a system that continues to result in mental (depression, anxiety, low self-esteem) and physical (chronic health challenges) damages (Bowen-Reid & Harrell, 2002; Williams, Neighbors, & Jackson, 2003), although we attempt to ignore it. Racism causes Blacks to remain at a disadvantage collectively although a few of us may feel as if we have *made it* because of our car, house, education, money, and/or employment status. This ideology of accomplishment based solely on material wealth causes some to adopt an individualistic purview, removing the innate communal orientation. Yet, as soon as any of us with wealth, fame, or prestige is removed from the environment where we hold rank, we become vulnerable to the full array of racism's manifestations. Thus, racism remains a chronic, but often silent, stressor for ALL Blacks regardless of status in this American country.

As a system, racism manifests itself as both covert (unknown) and overt (known) acts of discrimination (inequitable actions toward others based on race) and prejudice. Covert racism may be experienced in the workforce as a lack of equal employment opportunity and inequality in salary. For instance, being told we are over qualified and denied for employment positions in predominately White institutions, despite having the necessary qualifications and credentials. It may be displayed in the area of housing as discriminatory renting, loan inflation, and predatory lending for Blacks (Singleton, George, Dickstein, & Thomas, 2006). Additionally, covert racism may be exhibited in education in the form of discriminatory funding practices which results in disproportionate numbers of overcrowded classrooms, dilapidated buildings, and a shortage of current educational resources within the Black community. In terms of healthcare, an example of covert racism may be a lack of fresh produce and restaurants that serve healthy foods and overall inaccessibility to health lifestyle choices within the Black community. These experiences of covert racism perpetuate because oftentimes we have no concrete data regarding the disparity in what we receive compared to our Caucasian counterparts. On the other hand, if the differences are known there remains ambiguity as to why the variance occurred. When rationales are provided they cause us to actually believe that the disparities are justifiable.

Overt racism may be experienced on an environmental level within communities and institutions. For instance, we often receive little to no help when entering department stores. We are followed in stores and while walking within the community. It may also be evidenced by being called racial or derogatory slurs, in addition to being harassed and brutalized because of our skin tone. For example, driving an expensive car, being pulled over and told we or the car look like a vehicle identified in an illegal act. Thus, we are handcuffed and treated as a criminal based on insufficient evidence. In addition, we are belittled when asked how the car was obtained. Overt racism may also be experienced within the socio-political arena. For instance, there was minimal to no reprimand for any politician and news media personnel for the racist cartoon images, statements, and jokes directed towards President Obama. Additionally, there were no efforts to decrease and/or discontinue the public rallies organized with the intent of doing damage mentally and physically to the first Black President & family. This was said to simply be acts of freedom of speech.

The examples noted above are just a few illustrations to shed light on the chronic, covert and overt acts of racism in America that are minimally challenged. Because this array of experiences of racial injustices is often unchallenged collectively, overtime many adopt these manifestations of racism as the norm and fail to educate the next generation of the necessity to work together to end racism's toxic influence. As a result, Blacks develop an internalized oppressed mentality, which has proven to be most damaging, perpetuating the genocide of the Black community. As depicted within the following diagram, internalized oppression is a result of racism in which the prejudice thoughts and discriminatory behaviors regarding worth are accepted to be valid and warranted.

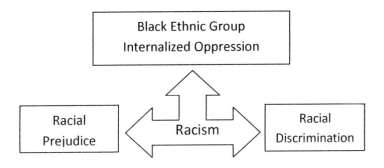

More specifically, internalized oppression is when we accept the negative messages about our community and incorporate those messages into our belief systems and behaviors. This belief system becomes the roadmap guiding our walk on life's journey, which we reciprocally communicate to our children, family, and community. Such is damaging to the Black community because it causes a limited outlook on life and our collective potential. Additionally, it removes communal thinking regarding families and community, and institutes a devalued sense of self resulting in Black self hate. Some of these negative messages are as follow:

1) Blacks are too limited in intellect to own the creative outlets or sports venues in which they participate.

2) Blacks do not read, therefore if your want to keep information from them, put it in a book.

3) Blacks are lazy, they don't want to work. Blacks rather collect welfare and have lots of children.

4) Blacks use the myth of racism as an excuse for limited social and economic progress.

5) Blacks are uncivilized beings.

Internalized oppression contributes to the disconnection among Blacks; we often interact with each other as persecutors rather than ally. Embraced negative messages have caused a wide-spread Black self hate resulting in many of the tragedies witnessed within various communities to this date (murders, robberies, drug deals, etc.). For instance, some have adopted a self-focused disposition which makes it extremely easy to degrade each other, deface our communities, and physically cripple and kill each other. Black students who choose to apply themselves within academia are accused of *acting White* by other Blacks. This results in the individual purposefully failing classes to be accepted and/or ostracizing themselves leading to low self-esteem. Reading is often seen as taboo or *not cool* and many think it is cool to resort to slang to express a thought. Furthermore, because of the resulting self hate associated with internalized oppression, some choose the slow kill of drug and alcohol abuse and risky sexual behaviors. Additionally, some minimize and ignore opportunities that aid in our ability to reach our fullest potential, or self actualization. For those fortunate to achieve success, many fail to support our Black youth and equip them with the tools to reach theirs.

These atrocities place limitations on ourselves and on our community allowing the negative and untrue messages of what it means to be Black to continue without challenge. This state of internalized oppression keeps us divided because we feel that we must escape or leave our community behind in order to be successful and *make it.* We preoccupy ourselves with our socioeconomic status, neighborhoods with gates and homeowners associations, social status, and acquired trinkets. While these things are important for matters of safety and prosperity, they also

6

serve as a distraction from our advancement as a collective in this country, our communities, and our youth. We need to acknowledge and understand how the system and our illness of internalized oppression work to captivate us, but also keep us at a disadvantage and divided.

How do we as Blacks embrace this communal orientation once again and work to eradicate the impact of racism and ultimately our internalized oppression? *First*, understand that our history was a collective experience which continues to impact us all. *Secondly*, take some time to understand the ways in which the system of racism works to keep us in bondage mentally, physically, and financially resulting in our division as a collective. Look at the influence of the racist system in your immediate and then the larger community. *Third*, position yourself to demonstrate greatness by committing to remain determined, ignoring society's negatives about our potential, embracing our creativity, and supporting each other's efforts to be great. *Fourth,* understand that our community's problems directly and indirectly are our individual problems. Therefore, we must no longer turn a blind eye or deaf ear to the troubles that consume our communities.

Internalized oppression results from this chronic system of racism (overt and covert), which corrodes the psyche of its rich communal energies, aborting our innate interdependent spirit. Use the words within this book to think about what you could do to assist in the individual and collective efforts of the Black community to reduce the impact of racism, both conscious and subconscious. The following letters depict our symptoms manifestation of internalize oppression. Each letter offers solutions for healing, growth, and means to resume our innate communal energies which will provide a solid platform for becoming triumphant over this racist plague that mentally and physically oppresses our communities for generations.

To the Collective

Why the Struggle Continues: A Psychological Perspective

Often times we conceptualize racism and its systemic structure as external. We tend to focus more on the appearance of the community, the amount of police brutality, lack of adequate housing, and educational opportunities for Black children compared to their Caucasian counterparts. However, how many can actually say that they have taken the time to consider the psyche of racism? Specifically, how many have assessed the psychological changes of a people over time as a result of years of disadvantages via a racist system. If such was done on a mass level, the maladaptive psychological implantation of Willie Lynch's letter would have discontinued when slavery was abolished in 1865. Willie Lynch was a White slave owner in the 1700's, who wrote a letter to instruct other slave owners about how to physically control and mentally manipulate African slaves in a way that would shackle them for generations. The method he used was fear of the White slave owner and division; between the self, the family, and community which resulted in a generational dependence on Whites for purpose, direction, opportunity, and worth.

Distorted cognition and negative behaviors do not change until individuals are convinced that their thoughts and behaviors are negatively impacting themselves and community. These cognitive and behavioral outcomes can be generational, passed from parent to offspring. Thus, it takes much work and several psychotherapeutic interventions to counteract this phenomenon. To reach our highest potential, the symbolic umbilical cord that nurtures generational negative beliefs about the self should be cut (see following diagram).

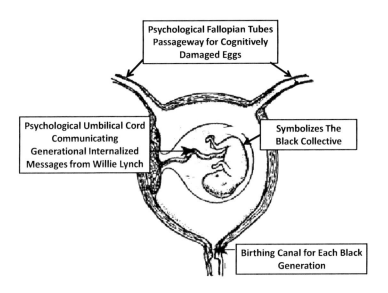

The diagram reflects psychological fallopian tubes, which provide passage for cognitively damaged eggs resulting from the historical implantations of Willie Lynch's Letter. After fertilization, the psychological umbilical cord continues to feed the fetus depreciating messages. The umbilical cord adds to progressive cognitive distortion as it provides additional ethnocentrically distorted messages about Bl ck experiences, value, and potential. The end result is generations of Blacks born with a distorted and psychologically crippled sense of self.

This psychological umbilical cord is so forcible that each generation is born with a collective lower self worth and amnesia regarding our history. Additionally, envy is displayed for those Blacks who choose to be different and soar beyond society's limitations. We have resorted to genocide as we emotionally abuse and physically murder Black children when historically we longed to hold them before the master sold them. Such is the reason why young boys join gangs in search of belongingness, value, and love, rather than a debate team. All of us know at least one Black who continues to greet others with "*What up my Nigga/Nigga Bitch?*"

We are content with not having businesses; however, the ones that are established are barely supported. The older generation defecates on the younger generation by failing to give them a chance to demonstrate their ability to be leaders and organizers of community change. This results out of jealously and inferiority complexes that their junior will be more successful at leading and organizing community efforts. We supposedly commemorate our historical accomplishments and struggle during Black History Month. However, the struggle will continue psychologically due to generational programming used to enslave each other.

Now, while the racist display of inequality is not as overt, the system continues to enslave minds as it did in the 1700's. This result causes a persistent and perpetual division of the family unit and community. To simplify, the Negro Overseer, the House Slave, and the Field Slave are concepts still held. The Negro Overseers are Blacks who are physically and emotionally cut off from other Blacks and community concerns. The House Slaves are Blacks who are able to "get by" due to status, accomplishments, and ability to cater to White interest. The Slaves working in the field are Blacks who struggle day to day to survive in this modern day racist society. Additionally, each time it is perceived that we have arrived, from integration to the present day of electing the first Black president, a complacent state of mind ensues. This complacency serves as a catalyst, forgetting that the struggle persists. It is almost as if the psychological umbilical cord connecting the psyche to Willie Lynch's letter damaged the hippocampus of the brain causing suffering from retrograde amnesia. It is the height of irony when standing, fist clutched in the air, to sing a hollow lyric of the Negro Anthem…

"We have come, over a way that which tears has been watered
We have come, treading our path through the blood of the
slaughtered
Out of the gloomy past, till now we stand at last…"

We attempt to suppress the echo of the ancestor's experiences and minimize the destructive nature of modern day racism. As long as we continue to suppress the ancestor's experiences and minimize our own, we will never reach our fullest potential. As Willie Lynch projected, the youth are still raised with a lack of self knowledge and Black men are continually told they are not needed. Additionally, others are continually allowed to discount racism as the cause of numerous maladies in the community. Now the word of God indicates that *"A people Perish for their Lack of Knowledge"*. However, we perish when pretending to forget, mismanaging the knowledge of our collective experiences, and not allowing the children to learn their history.

How do we begin to rid this disease of the mind? One method used in clinical practice is called Cognitive-Behavioral Techniques. This type of therapy entails a significant amount of focus and challenge to ones' thoughts in order to implement behavioral change. So in order to mentally cut the psychological umbilical cord feeding Willie Lynch's messages, the challenge is as follows:

What could be done differently that would demonstrate a level of appreciation for ancestors? Think about their experiences, struggles and sacrifices for the generations of grandparents, parents, and present day and those to come. Keep in mind, without the ancestor's efforts, present opportunities would not exist. Look beyond the societal limitations ascribed to Black people. Dream big, but allow those dreams to be realistic and obtainable. Be willing to make sacrifices to reach goals, but not at the expense of the community. Always remember to be a person who is determined to soar, yet remain one who knows how to lend a hand to their fellow man once reaching the predetermined destination.

Get past only knowing and recognizing those influential persons that the oppressor chooses to acknowledge, celebrate, and coin as great. Take a moment to research historical Black persons who pursued your field of interest. If aspiring to be a Postal Worker, know who was the first Black postal worker and their experience. Take a moment to examine the words used to embrace your fellow brother, sister, and children. What does the dictionary say it means? Is the definition meant to be positive or degrading? Now attempt to come up with a new, but positive word to embrace friends and family, but be sure to make it cool. Why should we continue to address a group of friends and family with, "What's up my nigga?" Literally what we are saying is, "What's up you ignorant person?" Last, but not least, make it a priority to teach and instill in your children a sense of ethnic pride. Don't raise them to internalize societal negative messages that Blacks are inferior, lazy, and only good for entertaining.

To eradicate the psychological struggles as a result of racial oppression and internalization, cut the psychological connection of Willie Lynch. Starting with the five general solutions above, can be the beginning of the healing process. This will afford the motivation, insight, and opportunity to resume needed efforts to become an independent people of economic, psychological, and societal wealth. There is much work to do. The words written in this letter are just the beginning. Are you up to the challenge?

From Nigger to What's Up My Nigga

"Nigger, come fetch me some water!"; "Nigger, where is my dinner?"; "Nigger, do as I say or I will lynch you in front of your wife and children!"; "Nigger, Nigger, Nigger!"...

We have been treated as less than human due to the color of our skin, texture of our hair, fullness of our lips, and broadness of our nose. Animals were given better care and living conditions. Based on physical characteristics we were considered inferior, uneducable, ignorant, and any other name that is degrading and instituted with the ability to captivate our psyche and mentally cripple us for centuries. Thus, each Black generation is birthed with a devalued since of ancestry, self, and ethnicity.

Due to physical and cultural differences we were enslaved and used to tend to the land, home, and children of Whites. Nevertheless, slavery was nothing new to the human race. However, the conditions under which Black ancestors served were inhumane; from sexual victimization, public lynching, brutal whippings, to the separation and destruction of the Black family. Although it is written that slavery was legally abolished January 31, 1865 (ratified 12/31/1865) via the 13 Amendment of the US constitution, the uncivil, inhumane, and unjust racial acts continued. Comparing the acute physical conditions and abuse, to the chronic psychological impact experienced from enslavement, it may be befitting to suggest that the psychological traumatic impact was more profound. The negative messages from the racist psychological abuse were ingrained into our bloodstream and continue to emerge with a lowering sense of ethnocentrism (ethnic pride) upon every generation birthed. From the ancestors to the present, we increasingly continue to view our lives based on the limiting standards that were designed to keep us inferior. Such results in many establishing goals based on an alleged infinitesimal worth and opportunities set by the oppressor. This lends evidence as to why, although great inventions came from us, as a collective we don't acknowledge them, or the inventors. The end result is the youth continue to be raised to settle for being great in the arts, rather than mathematics, science, and language.

Our ancestors heard on a daily basis the word, "Nigger" as if it was a greeting like Sir or Madam. "Nigger" is a word instituted to implement division and cause generations of inferiority complexes. "Nigger" is a word instituted to cause us to feel a combination of debasement, self hatred, and fear of the slave owner. "Nigger" *is* a word that should not be used to address a people who birthed mankind. "Nigger" is a word that should not be used to address a people who lived as Kings and Queens. "Nigger" is a word that should not be used to address a people who created and utilized science before science became known to man.

The word "Nigger" continued during the overt period of segregation in America from the 1950s—1970s. This period was comprised with organized marches, boycotts, and non-violent protest which were the hallmark of the Civil Rights movement. As a result, the appearance of racism began to modify the more the ancestors protested. During the day, our ancestors experienced racist directives dictating where they could dine, drink fountain water, sit, and receive education. Signs read for Colored/Negro and for White. However, throughout the night our ancestors experienced secret and brutal acts of persecution, preventing adequate sleep or no place to sleep as homes were often burned down. The brutality continued and discrimination in education, housing, and employment continued to persists, resulting in the younger generation during the 1960s developing a new movement; Black Power!

"Say it loud, I'm Black & I'm Proud!" The Black Power Movement was supported by ancestors who felt as if the non-violent acts of the Civil Rights Movement were not creating change regarding our community concerns quick enough. Thus, some banded together to develop an ALL Black activist organization. The Movement was in response to the period's rampant acts of police brutality. However, the momentum of the movement grew to embrace the sense of self, encouraging a communal sense of ethnic pride and self-esteem. The Black Power Movement of the 1960s encouraged Blacks to take responsibility for their lives and to be present in their communities by supporting Black leaders, businesses, and ideologies. The advent of the movement also led to a rejection of the slave era designations 'Nigger' and 'Negro' and gave rise to people of African descent renaming themselves BLACK.

Black pride elicited a sense of hope that life could be better during harsh and debilitating times. Opportunities were in the making, some aspects of life were changing, and Black ethnocentrism emerged once again. We recognized that we deserved better than what society offered. Our ancestors went from holding their heads down to walking upright with chins and heads up. The physical appearance of the Black man & woman was once again embraced. Afros and the coils of the hair were loved; fullness of the lips and hips were celebrated; and the sway of our walk was revered.

We went from being degraded by an oppressive system, to having Black leaders assist with our initial emancipation. However, a few collective accomplishments resulted in a complacent state of mind. Our collective accomplishments, coupled with complacency caused a mass illusion that Blacks have arrived and all aspects of life were now just and appropriate. Complacency resulted in the fight for complete liberation coming to an end because of the first few accomplishments on the agenda (ability to vote, desegregation, etc.). Yes we can vote, obtain education at White schools, overt segregation was eliminated, and Blacks no longer have to ride the back of mass transit. Yet, because a few were able to obtain much of life's liberties as their Caucasian counterparts, the enthusiasm to collectively fight for justice remains obsolete. The collective forgot and lost the enthusiasm to continue to fight for justice for other aspects of life. As result, we still are covertly discriminated against in housing, loans, education, healthcare, and employment opportunity.

A few from the Black collective have acquired a car, home, education, and status, but the majority did not. This counterfeit *elite group* is then ostracized, adapts to the oppressor's mentality and begins to contribute to the debasement of the Black collective. Some sit back and watch others who look like them struggle. We now, more dangerously than ever before, stand divided as a people based on the standards of the oppressor that have been embraced as the way of life. We fought to eliminate the limitations placed on us as a people, but once eliminated, our ignorance within group allowed them to be reestablished. Advancement is minimized, degraded and blocked by not embracing each other's accomplishments and acquired skills.

We have moved from ethnic pride to ethnic hate. No longer embracing our African descent but, coveting our brothers and sisters' individual accomplishments. We make fun of each other regarding skin tone, hair texture and facial features, and consider the pursuit of excellence as "acting white". We have poisoned our psyche by allowing society's standards and ideologies to become our way of life. Not remembering that these things were implemented to keep us at a disadvantage in a multitude of ways from economics to housing. Thus, we positioned ourselves to once again depend on the majority in this country for leadership and life purpose. We settled for what opportunities were given. We settled as entertainers. However, that entertainment was at our expense. In an attempt to make society laugh, they laughed at the ignorance of Blacks who made fun of all the crippling things from slavery to the captivation of our psyche. The very situations that ended in brutal deaths, we MOCK.

A few eventually flourished in the entertainment industry because we belittled ourselves for money; making society laugh not with us, but at us for monetary gain. It became okay to degrade our Africanness; our dark skin, our coiled hair, our full lips, and our oppressive experiences. This distorted sense of success began in comedy. But is now evidenced in the jobs we settle for and some of the words we speak, including the lyrics of rap artist and our daily communication when interacting with each other.

What do you say when people take the experiences that once victimized them and use it to entertain a world that continues to see them as less than? Our historical experiences have caused our psyche to function in a state of mental suffering where we do not understand the consequences and appropriateness of our actions and have an inability to care and prepare for self and future generations. Presently, although some youth and adults may greet each other with "***What's up my Nigga***", resulting in the stomachs of others turning. It can be understood why the very word that is associated with years of victimization is now minimized, embraced, and mocked. As a result of years of physical and continued mental enslavement, we suffer from a distorted sense of self and people. The end result is countless maladies including the use of degrading words to greet one another to a complacent stance regarding continued limitations placed on us.

What's the solution to this collective dilemma? We must work to remember our historical experiences. Additionally, we must remember that although some of us and our parents were not physically enslaved or experienced overt racist acts, OUR GRANDPARENTS, GREAT GRANDPARENTS, or GREAT-GREAT GRANDPARENTS DID! We must take a few minutes to imagine what life was like for our ancestors and realize that we are still placed at a disadvantage due to the covert forms of systemic racism. Therefore, we can begin to consider the rationale why our continued use of self-devaluing behaviors should cease. If not, ignorance will continue to serve as the catalyst that aids in the perpetual destruction of generations. We need to remember and be realistic, we do not have complete liberation yet…IT'S IMPORTANT TO REMEMBER OUR COLLECTIVE EXPERIENCES PAST & PRESENT!

The Comedy Show

As Blacks, we often experience situations that can make us question whether or not the situation was purposely racially charged. In such situations, there may be a feeling of helplessness being that there remains ambiguity about the underlying reason for its occurrence. Here's an example…

I went to a comedy show during February, Black History Month. It was the first show and the crowd was small, possibly 15-20 people; four of which were Black, including myself and a friend. The majority were Caucasian and Latino. I walked out due to the tasteless, bigoted remarks made by the White male Emcee as he introduced the third comedian.

The comedy show was held in an extremely small area of the lower level of this establishment. Therefore, my friend and I chose not to sit in our assigned front row seating area as it was directly on top of the small 4X5 ft stage. The Emcee returned to the stage and said *"Why did they seat the two Black people in the back, isn't it Black History month. You know I love Karaoke, but I cannot do it to rap music because I can't say a certain word."* He proceeded off the stage and pointed his microphone to a Caucasian woman and asked *"What word is it? You can't say it either!"* Another Caucasian woman from the back blurted out, *"You can say it as long as you place an 'a' at the end; NIGGA!"*

I immediately became infuriated and blurted out, *"Not every Black person is fond of the N-word regardless of an 'a' or 'er' at the end; it's a demonstration of ignorance."* As I proceeded to gather my coat and walk out to speak with the manager, I was greeted with more ignorance as she defended the comedian, saying that she did not believe the Emcee meant any negativity by his comments.

Regardless, the joke was disrespectful both as a paying patron and as part of the collective. Here are some questions pondered at the end of this experience.

1. Have we positioned ourselves to provide the world opportunity to reverse the standards our ancestors fought hard to obtain by the negative words and behaviors we choose to use in interacting with one another?

2. Have we made it acceptable for others to publicly degrade us, both covertly and overtly?

Economics: Why Those on Top Stay There

From the creation of mankind to the present, there have been divisions among people. Division based on an array of differences resulted in a multitude of maladies, including the oppression of those classified as the minority in this country, Black people. Differences in regard to language, skin tone, birth place, and culture were considered evidence of deficiency. We were coined as an inferior species based on these differences. Despite these alleged deficiencies that aided in the perception of Blacks as mentally weak, the ancestors were deemed physically strong enough to be slaves of Caucasians' land and property. Blacks were made to build and cultivate Caucasians' land, yet prohibited from obtaining the skills to become economically free. Although the times have changed and we are not legally prohibited from reading, we continue to experience disadvantages that impact opportunity to obtain wealth and knowledge.

Such resulted in Caucasians developing and maintaining a sense of superiority as they continued to withhold information. Our Black ancestors were denied opportunities to learn, placing them at a social, financial, and psychological disadvantage that evidenced itself from generation to generation. However, there were a few ancestors who stole and snuck opportunities to learn. As some began to obtain knowledge, they began to view themselves as an elite and selective group. Unfortunately, many of those few also adopted the individualistic posture of Caucasians. They kept the knowledge for self, rather than sharing with the larger community. This lack of shared knowledge also inhibited economic growth. Due to this lack of shared knowledge, the community stays at a disadvantage. Nevertheless, Caucasians continue to work together sharing knowledge and creating economic opportunity. Thereby, Caucasians are placed in a position to remain on top of the economic ladder while Blacks remain economically oppressed having chosen not to financially empower ourselves. If those who have been privy to the underground railroad of Caucasian wealth building would ablaze the pathway for those who were left behind, then we could all enjoy benefits of economic liberation.

The underground railroad of Caucasian wealth building entails specific principles that have been grafted onto their economic DNA of every new generation. They are as followed:

1. Education is non-negotiable. Children are propelled toward academic excellence. They are expected to be the owners, investors, and leaders of their community.

2. The understanding of social and historical context is non-negotiable. Caucasian children cut their teeth on the accomplishments and traditions of their people.

3. Monetary wisdom is non-negotiable. Caucasian children are taught economic formulas. These formulas include an understanding that wealth is more than having cash at hand; rather it is knowing how economic systems work.

4. Generational wealth is non-negotiable. Caucasians view the transmission of wealth from generation to generation as essential to family survival.

In order to see economic freedom these principles must be adopted. Study these teachings until they become our new normal. Then graft these teaching onto the economic DNA of our children. Teach our children the difference between getting a job and living a career. Also, teach our children the differences between the confines of cash and the wherewithal of wealth.

The psyche needs changing from the desperate belief of not having enough, to the liberated posture of economic empowerment. With this new power, a new destiny is created, positioning future generations to be economically free and self sufficient. This will position Blacks to no longer be on the bottom of the economic growth ladder, but equally aligned, if not greater than the oppressor.

Am I My Brother's Keeper?

Am I My Brother's Keeper (from Genesis 4:9) was the theme of a talk I gave at an annual Martin Luther King, Jr. Commemoration at a historical Black church in Western Pennsylvania. The chapter from Genesis illustrates the story of Cain and Abel. Cain was filled with jealousy and anger because of his brother, Abel's accomplishment, which lead to murdering this favored brother. Cain's motives behind killing his brother Abel, applies to the current predicament of the Black community.

Am I my brother's keeper…this scripture reflects two opposing mentalities. As Abel becomes successful and surpasses Cain in life's opportunities, his accomplishments began to elicit jealousy, resentment, and even homicidal behavior in Cain. This display of negative emotions can be seen within our communities. As some attempt to advance in education and career, others discredit those positive efforts. Coincidentally, there are reports in the news media about the increase of homicide, primarily by our hands against brothers and sisters in the neighborhood.

Martin Luther King, Jr. stated in his *Letter from Birmingham Jail*, April 16, 1963, "the oppressed people cannot remain oppressed forever; that the yearning for freedom will eventually manifest itself". During the 1960's, Dr. King and other social activists led the Black community in challenging the country's unjust overt laws and practices. This movement served as a catalyst for national changes in federal and state laws. While they worked to end segregated facilities from education to public transportation, the segregated mentality of the oppressor continued and the oppressor made changes too.

The institution of racism and the behaviors of its proponents became covert in the Black community. The institutionalized expressions of the racist mindset became more difficult to discern as we integrated. Particularly, when some advanced and "made it", while others continued to reap hardship.

Furthermore, within Dr. King's letter, he wrote that the oppressed people "have many pent up resentments and latent frustrations, and they must release them. If the repressed emotions are not released in nonviolent ways, they will seek expression through violence". I interpret this to mean Blacks initially had feelings of resentment toward the oppressor due to experiences of mental and physical brutality. However, these deeply rooted feelings towards the oppressor were never released appropriately and fully. The end result is the birth of internalized oppression.

Can you begin to see the foundation for the present crisis? How this scripture applies to the current condition of the Black nation? Biblical history attests that when people are subjected to division, the result is competition. Generational seeds of competition, coupled with years of enslavement, onset the rage initially aimed at the oppressor. However, what happens when the object of that anger is unknown? The oppressor was clever. He created methods that would cause years of division based on illusive and meaningless differences. Such division was put in place and carried out for generations by tactics, including the Willie Lynch letter. Recall, the Willie Lynch Letter (see page 10 for summation of the Willie Lynch Letter) discloses a slave owner's rules on how to keep an African shackled not only physically, but mentally. This mental enslavement has presented itself to be most damaging.

With the oppressor's clever structures many are often unsure, if they are actually experiencing racism because its manifestations have changed. Its appearance has moved from the obvious to the unknown and the unknown at times, is a very scary and confusing place. The unknown can raise questions if there is even a cause to fight for. It causes individuals to diminish efforts for assuring a positive change that impacts the collective. The unknown causes removal from the communal thinking of the ancestors to the individualistic thinking of the oppressor and asks "what is on my personal agenda". It causes a focus on the differences between the fellow man, rather than his advancement.

The mind's complex but faulty mechanism has allowed us to be lulled by a few collective accomplishments. Not being able to decipher after the efforts of the Civil Rights Movement which actions are racist and which are not, has left the community in such distress. After all of the marches, boycotts, and sit-ins, some positive change has led to the delusion that Blacks are actually free. That there is actually a fair and equal opportunity in this land called America; that we can obtain the same as our Caucasian counterparts, with the same efforts. Oh, the mind is such a complex, but faulty mechanism. The presentation of racism has changed and is now evidenced in what is called modern-day racism. There are no more signs telling us where we cannot go and where we are not allowed. Reports of daily lynchings are not whispered about in church circles. Modern day racism entails clever and covert policies to keep us from receiving all that the state and federal laws suggests a citizen should obtain. Clever! So clever that some begin to forget our history and the preciousness of the Civil Rights legacy.

Instead, the achievements of our brother and sister are coveted. Have you ever been asked with an incredulous disbelief, "how did you get that job; how did you get that car; how did you get to go to that school; how did you get to own a house?" It is almost as if you did not work for and deserve what was obtained.

Stuck in a morass of subconscious envy, we look at our brother, and ask "why do you have and I have not?" Yet, we are still carrying around repressed generational rage directed towards the oppressor for years of struggle. This deeply rooted repressed rage begins to surface. What happens when the individual you are angry at is unclear? Or if he is known, he is difficult to capture because he is not one, but many. He is not a man but a system, a structure. What do you do? At whom do you direct this pent up frustration? What happens is that frustration becomes displaced. It is released on your brother or sister, who has what you wish to obtain. What happens when you are angry? Do you think clearly? Do you process all of your actions and feelings? Oh, how clever was the oppressor! Our displaced anger has led to an individualistic and competitive thinking people who have lost the vision of the ancestors. We no longer fight daily for the advancement of our people; instead we fight each other for what the other has obtained. Unfortunately, when we do allow the spirit of our ancestors to mesh it is in response to a flagrant racial incident that has garnered national attention.

We have moved from being our brother's keeper to being our brother's competitor. When will we collectively take a stand to regain the communal vision of Toussiant L'Ouverture, Harriet Tubman, Marcus Garvey, Malcolm X, or Martin Luther King, Jr.? When will we collectively fight for the improved quality of our neighborhoods, for the education to our children, for the healthcare for our families, for adequate housing, and for equal employment opportunity? Why must the Black nation be a dysfunctional family that only gathers during funerals or moments of catastrophic crisis? What will it take to consistently strive and fight for positive changes that will impact our communities and the nation? What will it take? It seems today's continued racial profiling and the police brutality in every city and state is not enough. Beatings and acts of physical aggression in every city and state is not enough. Impoverished Black neighborhoods in every city and state are not enough. Inadequate education and healthcare facilities in every city and state is not enough. What will it take? How far back into a brutal history of racist persecution do we need to repeat? Is it that unclear or are we so far removed from the cause that it is easier to blame each other, rather than work together to end this racist system?

Are you your brother's keeper? Have you been? Do you at least aspire to be? I often ponder the communal drive and determination of our ancestors. How dismayed they must be at our ignoble condition watching from heaven's gates? The poison of racist mentalities has corrupted our hearts, minds, and souls. The enslaved Black mind is captured and blinded by false representations of freedom and fair opportunities within this so called land of the free. Yes, some may be able to eat from the finest restaurants and buy expensive materials. Some may have obtained higher education and had the opportunity to attend any college or university of choice. Some may have even married outside of the race with no threat of being beaten or lynched. However, is that all our ancestors fought for?

For some to have the opportunity to prosper and enjoy societal liberties, while others continue to struggle in a system that promotes and thrives off of failures. Does that make you your brother's keeper?

The false representation of freedom is an optical illusion which we tragically teach to our children. It is a mistaken belief that working hard, moving out of Black neighborhoods, and going to a White school means making it. Please! Removing yourself from the cause and your own people is not maintaining the legacy of the ancestors. Think about it. I can assure you that racial profiling doesn't care about the privilege of your address or the refinement of your *Caucasioned Diction* when you are driving in a particular neighborhood at the wrong time. There is more to the ancestor's legacy than this.

The ancestor's legacy will not be honored until we come together and work towards ending this segregationist structure called racism. After illustrating the origins of the problems the Black nation is facing, it would be remiss to not offer a new direction. Our ancestors created a legacy. But with prayer, hard work, and the renewing of minds, the legacy can continue and can accomplish its goals.

So how do we become "Our Brother's Keeper"? First, understand that the fight of our ancestors for humanity and justice for ALL is not over. The systemic structures put in place years ago are still a working force in this nation. Let us recall the failed rescue mission for the Katrina Hurricane victims. Recall the constant racist critiques against President Barack Obama. Recall the continued racial profiling and brutality targeting Black males. Do I need to go on? We need to understand the impact of how this multi-leveled system of racism operates.

Once we understand how the system works, we have to become more concerned about our brothers and sisters, rather than continuing the mentality of "I got mine, now you get yours". Make a commitment to renew individual minds with a transformed communal mindset. Many acquired education and experiences that could offer immeasurable benefit to the collective. Share the wealth, not only with your children, but the communal family. Work together to rebuild neighborhoods, rather than moving away as if that solves the painful problems of substandard housing and inadequate education. Organize to reduce the illegal drug activity, gang violence, and other acts of verbal and physical assault on the streets.

Teach our young people our history. Do not rely on the school system to teach the children our legacy, particularly when that discussion is relegated to the shortest month of the year. Children need to know that Black people were scientist, inventors, doctors, architects, and literary scholars. So they can aspire to do the same, rather than subscribing to the myth that they can only be athletes and entertainers. Encourage children to study, read, and pursue higher education. Take them to the library, the museum, and have play dates at book stores and cultivate their minds. Do not raise them to think, for a second, that where they are from can and will determine where they go.

Exorcise the belief that Black institutions are no longer good enough when, at one point, those precious institutions were the only ones that could be relied upon. It is essential to support and buy from Black businesses. Why spend money in places or on materials owned by people who could care less about our community and the issues that impact our people. Furthermore, there is nothing wrong with sending Black children to Historically

Black Colleges and University's (HBCUs). Those essential institutions foster a sense of family and communal concern. As a student comes to understand the history of HBCU's they develop a sense of pride in their heritage.

Brothers and sisters, we must Vote! Stop this negative thinking that my one effort will not make a difference. Vote in every election. Vote in every local, primary, and general election. Take someone you know does not vote to the polls. If we do not do this essential thing we will never stand firm on the ground of civil and social justice. It only takes one to take a stand to make a difference. Start this year, right now...

Am I my brother's keeper? Having seen the origins of the illness and its general impact along with a few solutions, what are you going to do? Allow this message to speak to you and be ye transformed by the renewing of your mind.

Embrace Your Junior

Why do some older adults fail to embrace the accomplishments of younger generations? Why is a young Black woman who realizes academic success often given a cold shoulder when seeking out the community's support? Why are young Black males disparaged by older Black men because they are brilliant? Ironically, when young adults determine to embrace the sacrifices of the Civil Rights Movement by adding their own accomplishments to its result, they are often treated as if they have done something wrong, almost blasphemous. Beyond that, they are told that they have no understanding of our peoples' struggle and their impact on today's social struggles is without applicable context.

What are the Young Gifted and Black (YGB) to do? The very people, the YGB are aiming to reach ignore them because they are young and new to their areas of expertise. How are the YGB supposed to develop greater skills if the community does not give them an opportunity? The unfortunate truth is that some members of the community family only respect the YGB brilliance when that brilliance is being vetted and fed at the Caucasian table. Why do we need the permission of the oppressor before embracing our own? For without the continued generational exchange of knowledge, the community will perish allowing our collective brilliance to rot away.

Many older adults actively choose not to share from the well of their experiential insights and believe that to do so would somehow risk their position in the community hierarchy. They believe that if they had to struggle, then any young person with a fancy degree and who "thinks they know something" should have to struggle too. This "since I had to" mentality is just another unfortunate manifestation of our people's history of oppression. The unfortunate and tragic truth is that it divorces our YGB from the apprenticeship of those who should be their cultural mentors. Furthermore, that same oppressive history has left us so psychically eroded that oftentimes the community self-righteously rejects the essential role of our YGB in the formula for complete liberation. These self centered ideologies, nurtured by the dogmas of jealousy and selfishness, adversely impact the advancement of the entire collective. The end product of this symptom is the perpetual generational decline in the collectives' potential to be a community of influence. For if the YGB's experiential ideologies are put to service, the collective will be in a position to prevail, reorganizing and instituting policies that produce wealth. This will seat the collective at the table of leadership, no longer dependent on a system that works to our extinction.

It's time to put the inferiority complexes aside and embrace the YGB, as the older adults need someone to pass their knowledge onto. Don't perceive the YGB as competition. The older adults' role now is to assist in keeping their desired legacy alive and to do such they need someone YGB to pass the torch of knowledge and skill. The Black Community still needs much, so don't block the YGB from leading and continuing the fight for advancement as a people.

The sanction of racist ideologies has caused division among the older and younger generations. This symptomatic manifestation of the "since I had to" mentality, contributes to our illness of internalized oppression. Older adults need to reckon the vitality of informational wealth interdependence; as for without it, we will lie breathless in this world that is forever evolving.

Remove your ego…

EMBRACE YOUR JUNIOR!

To my Brothers

Daddy Where Are You?

"Why don't you pick up when I call? How come you never come when you say you are on your way? Where are you daddy? Can you take me to the park? Can you pick me up from school? Can you call me?"

These are the spoken, and often unspoken, questions of children without their biological father's presence. Brother, you loved the loving the woman gave you; whether planned or unexpected a child was conceived. Brother when the relationship does not last, why often time is it at the child's expense? Leaving the child with the spoken and unspoken question...*Daddy where are you?* Children often experience low self-worth, depression, and tend to blame themselves for their father's absence. Such leads to several self-devaluing behaviors, including social isolation, negative peer interactions (engaging in bullying), lack of focus on academics, and an infinitesimal view of their future.

Fathers, who are influential and active, often have children who are able to witness and value the significance of a Black male's presence. They come to rely on him for direction, love, support, and protection; positioning them to navigate some of the negatives regarding Black father's as they mature. Our sons are able to have a positive male figure to emulate. Daughters will have a Black male who shows her how to present herself as a woman, in addition to teaching her how a man should treat her. Our children who don't have their father's present are deprived of this parental dynamic that is essential to their development.

Why is it so easy to turn your back on an innocent child who did not ask to be born? Is the life that you helped bare not as important as yours? This letter is directed to men who simply woke up one day and said they wanted to be free of responsibility. Free with no concern for the child that longs for them. What type of man walks out on his child during the years he needs him most? This individual must be self-absorbed. He is a child himself psychological. He may even think it is cool or think it makes him a man to say "Yo, I got Jane pregnant or I have children". Immaturity minimizes a man's value if he chooses to engage in committed sexual intimacy. He places notches on his belt as he "scores" with women, irresponsibly aiding in baring life with no intent to nurture the child. Nevertheless, being the catalyst which causes our youth to grow up without a strong Black male's presence is wicked. Such is one reason why some of our youth look to outside forces (gangs, drugs, and acting out behaviors) for love and acceptance. They also look to romantic relationships and sex before they are psychologically and emotionally mature enough to cope with the idiosyncrasies of these interpersonal interactions. As a result they are emotional, physically, and psychologically abused. This robs children of their youth, which aids in them developing a limited outlook on life and their future potential.

Brother, take a second to think about the damage you are enabling. Your child needs love, protection, and encouragement. If time is needed to get your life together, communicate such. But don't allow your absence to be forever. For instance, position yourself to have something influential to offer; communicate what is going on in your personal life. Let the rationale for your short-term absence be known. Your energy is needed in the community. The children, home, and community are in better standing with your presence, as you are a brave warrior on the frontline of each of societal obstacles leading us to victory. When the question "daddy where are you?" rises again, the response needs to be "I am on my way".

Brother, divorce the individualistic ideologies resulting from our illness of internalized oppression which affects the psyche, eliciting the need to separate yourself. This need to flee arises from the fears and frustrations experienced as a Black man trying to survive in a racist society. Additionally, you experience these emotions trying to engage and navigate interpersonal relationships with some women who have been trained to minimize the importance of your presence. However, work to reinstitute yourself within the community and resume your role as leader and protector. You may believe you do not know how to be a father because yours was not present. Be different than what you had growing up. Comprehending the significance within a child's life and understanding that without a father's presence they may be malnourished, will warrant a willingness to fulfill your duty.

There is no manual on how to be a parent. But the best way to start is to be present with a positive attitude and honor your word. Remember the feeling when, after waiting with excitement, your father failed to show after making plans. Children need to hear that they are valued by their parents because if not that void will be filled by the streets that most often aim to use them. Do not allow money or time to ever be an excuse as there are always free things to do. Above everything else, your child comes first.

Take a stand to be present; make an effort to call regularly. No minutes on the phone; drop an e-mail or text. Make time on the weekend, if even for a few hours. Ask about school; particularly grades, strengths, and challenges. Ask about their peers, teachers, and aspirations. This is a start to show you care and value their life, education, and future. Your excuse may be *"I don't have any money"*. The solution to that is to walk them to school or pick them up. This gives you time to talk. Although you may not have received it, give your child a hug and tell them you love them.

If this message does not affect your heart and change your behavior; many children are destined for destruction. If this symptom of our illness remains untreated, we are facilitating the seduction of children by the gangs that hold the streets and schools hostage. We are creating a generation of emotionally asphyxiated adults who raise their children without love, protection, and standards. We are commissioning portraits of low expectation and diminished self-esteem to our young people. In essence, with every discarded, abandoned, or ignored child we are aborting our people's bountiful destiny. The existence of our people is predicated on the strength, leadership, and protection of the men. In other words brother, we need you to survive. *Daddy Where Are You?* We need you to come home soon!

Young Man, Pants Up!

Young Brother the world is not interested in seeing your underwear! Walking within the community, there are a multiple amount of young brothers wearing their pants below their waist. Young brothers have transformed both unbefitting styles of dress and word usage. However, they have yet to fathom the consequences of this causeless concession of style of dress.

Why are your pants down in this 21st century? You constantly have to pull them up or waddle wide-legged to keep them from falling down. You wear your pants everyway but up; below the waist, at the thigh or even more outrageously, hanging just above the knee. What are you trying to say dressing this way? Do you know the history of the pants hang low phenomenon? Do you understand the messages being sent when carrying yourself this way? Some say the style has its origins in the prison culture. In jail, prisoners are not allowed to wear belts, because they could be used to hang themselves or strangle another inmate. Beyond that it is said that prisoners wear their pants sagging off their behinds to signal to other inmates that they are available for prison sex.

At what age does it stop? What careers will allow such a dress code? What type of women are you attempting to attract? What type of crowd are you signaling you wish to belong to? Unfortunately, being Black and a male, caution must be excised regarding presentation. The world views this form of dress as associated with negative behaviors, including gang activity and drug dealing. Despite the manner of dress, you are likely to be a target. Wearing sagging pants will increase that susceptibility to profiling, harassment and brutality.

Since childhood I was encouraged to dress for the future I was working to create. Can you imagine the manifestations that would occur if your dress was as big as your possibility and promise? The truth is, when presenting ourselves based on aspiration, we work harder to make certain that vision is accomplished. Another inescapable truth is that people judge physical presentation. Wear a belt! You can still rock the loose or baggy fit.

Be encouraged to walk with soul. Walk with your head high. Pants don't have to be mid thigh to be cool. Make your own fashion statement. Display brilliance instead of boxers. Show the world your power.

PULL YOUR PANTS UP.

THE WORLD IS NOT INTERESTED IN SEEING YOUR UNDERWEAR!

Can A Brother Get A Break?

The world will view you as a threat, whether light-skin, brown-skin, or dark-skin; whether jeans or a suit and tie. The soul and rhythm of your walk causes the oppressor to feel inferior as he subconsciously hears the beat of the African drum in each foot step. It's a walk that signifies strength and triumph over the racist plague that attempted to slaughter Blacks for generations. Whether you have high school, trade school, or college education, many will attempt to discredit any knowledge brought to an establishment. The media shows thugs, womanizers, or drug dealers. However, so many still fight to establish this so-called American dream; accomplishing educational goals and establishing meaningful careers. Working hard is a daily occurrence, but seemingly unappreciated at work and home. Understand there is no break because the oppressor has coined you as subservient and has taught women the means to emasculate you over generations. Because of this, the root of your frustration and fears are often ambiguous resulting in incongruent releases of animosity at the detriment of family and community. Once the collective understands this generational symptomatic toxic cycle, you will get a break.

Although attempting to walk, head held high, the weight of negative attacks places a hunch in your back causing your head to bow low. This affects the stride, reverting it to a stumble turning your rhythmic beat into BABEL. Ceaselessly there is a psychological struggle with low self worth, the hope for appreciation, impulses to flee from the community, and your instinct to care for your family. Yet daily there is a new attempt to start fresh. People may not want to speak or employ you because of their assumptions about the way you dress and wear your hair. Yet, when working hard, taking care of family, and accomplishing goals, you may go unnoticed or overlooked. Every time you do something wrong, regardless of how minor, not only are you placed in the media, but the entire Black male collective becomes suspect and endangered. When attempting to take time for self to increase opportunities, it is perceived as betrayal as if positioning oneself for progress and prosperity is breaking a rule. However, when remaining stagnant, maintaining a limited routine and taking on household responsibilities, there are infinitesimal accolades. It seems that regardless of what is done, so much attention is given to flaws, that the power of your potential is sometimes all but ignored. You are minimized, which cripples the self-esteem, and then many wonder why you keep quiet and rarely defend yourself. In bed, you're called "daddy", but day to day are told how much aggravation you cause.

Brother, know that there are some who actually appreciate you. Some are coming to understand that, regardless of what right you aim to do, others will always be suspicious of your potential to do wrong. In addition, the oppressor will always fear that you will disaffirm their diminutive view of your commissioned rich destiny. Some understand that you not only experience stress and anxiety at home, but also while walking the streets, because brother, strong presence causes society to feel inferior. Your build, tone, and stand remind the oppressor that all of their efforts to annihilate us miscarried. Although he presents to the world that your differences are deficits, subconsciously he knows that the dissimilarities make you predominant. When persons feel inferior they do whatever possible to counteract that feeling, giving them a sense of superiority. Therefore, in the home your manhood may be belittled and in the streets your Blackness is the unfortunate catalyst to ethnic profiling and violence.

So when do fathers, brothers, sons, and lovers get a break? The Black Man will get a break, when Black women embrace their accomplishments and flaws. We have to respect and celebrate our own before society will even consider changing their ideologies. Black women have to stop belittling our sons, which causes a stunt in their potential to be great Black men. Eliminate the negative name calling, exclusive focus on their challenges, lack of celebration of their accomplishments, minimizing their hurts, and minimizing their aspirations. Allow our sons to be youthful and enjoy childhood, rather than forcing them to take responsibility of us and our home. This stunts their growth and counterproductively transforms boys into men, to fill the selfish void for adult companionship. Additionally, discontinue placing minimalistic expectations on our sons, as we encourage them to engage in sports rather than nurturing their potential to be owners of corporations.

Embrace Black men and support them. They should be able to find the strength to travel on life's journey through the Black Women in their life. Speak life into their souls, pray for them, and their aspirations. Tell and show them they are needed and appreciated despite their shortcomings. Take time to listen to their day and offer a word or physical embrace of encouragement.

With regard to romantic partners, treat them with respect and honor, particularly those who show themselves as respectful. We need to learn how to be slow to speak, but quick to listen. We need to hear the Black Man in our life; understand his visions, his needs, and wants. If you have more degrees and money than him, don't use that as a means to stroke your own ego and emasculate him. Treat him as an equal, a partner, and allow him to be a MAN. Show him that that his presence, strength, ideas, and love are needed.

Create a safe place for him to come to when society, work, and the world beat him down because of the color of his skin. Hold him with a firm embrace and let him know you are there to assist him on his journey. Do not minimize his concerns, but validate his anxieties. Support his visions even without knowing its importance. We should not be an added stressor on his shoulders, reminding him of all the things yet to accomplish. We should not position ourselves to be his silent killer by the words we speak out of anger. Using words that psychologically whip him as if he was tied to a tree and given lash after lash until exhaustion. Words such as *"you're stupid", "don't even know why I deal with you", "you're worthless", and "I don't need you"* eventually become the seeds of thought planted in the heart, which will cause us to then act out.

Our oppressive experiences have generationally trained the psyche to minimize the importance of Black men within the home and community. As with our each symptom expressed throughout this book, we must understand our behavioral manifestation and its maladaptive impact. Support and respect Black males, both young and old because their presence remains the backbone of our collective survival.

To my Sisters

Sister, Allow Your Child's Father to Be There

This letter is tailored to a relationship that failed between two fairly decent adults. However, the woman is choosing not to allow the father to be active in the life of the children. This letter is not tailored to women whose man was physically abusive and for safety reasons it is best that, in those situations, there is minimal contact. Nor is it directed towards women whose man just walked out without no contact to be found.

Unfortunately, women scorned from an unsuccessful relationship can turn bitter. This sourness results from the termination of the current relationship that elicits suppressed thoughts and emotions from past unfulfilling parental, romantic, or platonic exchanges. In an effort to assure that this deprivation does not occur again, to self or children, relational difficulties are often resolved with a complete repudiation of men. This bitterness massages the wounds from past devastating interactions and negatively influences future relationships at our expense, which also affects the children's relationships. While a relationship is in progress, the man's faults are minimized or excuses are made. Nevertheless, once the relationship is over, he is often called many derogatory names. The tensions between parents trickle into the child's interaction with both parents. However, if the mother solely raises the children and the tension remains, oftentimes the children have an estranged relationship with the father for several reasons.

One reason is some women lie about the whereabouts of the father. Since we do not want him anymore, we immaturely do not want the children with him either. **Secondly**, some women outright ask the biological fathers to relinquish their parental rights. **Third**, some women relocate far enough where there can only be minimal contact. At the time of estrangement some are so wounded, we act selfishly, misconstruing these behaviors as forms of emotional protection for self and child. However, such has a detrimental impact on a child's psyche, self-esteem, and sect of interpersonal relationships. We have no clue what potential confusion and damage this may cause to our children. **Fourth,** and possibly the most detrimental, are that some raise a child to believe that their biological father is 'dead'. Died while the child was an infant, yet the biological father is alive and desiring contact to no avail.

The above four rationales are most damaging if there is no positive Black male father figure to fill this void in the form of a new boyfriend or stepfather. If neither is available, then an uncle or grandfather can help. Some women honestly believe we do best by raising a child without a father figure's influence. Although many may attempt to do such, there are still frailties associated with the Black father's absence. Every Black child needs a strong Black male present within their life. Generally, a man is needed to teach a boy child how to be a man and a man is needed to teach a young girl how a man should treat her.

Specifically, a positive Black man can teach sons how to grow and develop into a strong Black man. With their guidance, sons will be taught how to have a back bone, a mind of their own, to be independent, reliable, goal driven, and have influence within the community. Strong Black men can also teach their sons how to be the head of the household, not just financially, but to protect, love, guide, and respect their family. Most important, they are the only ones who can teach sons the continued experiences of racial oppression and its infestation on the Black man. They can raise sons to be knowledgeable and watchful of the ways in which the systemic structures of racism attempt to attack and discredit the Black man. Thus, positioning our sons to be one step above, therefore they can grow and rise above the oppressive acts taking heed to their father's experiences and teachings.

Positive Black men are needed to teach daughters how they should complement a Black man. A Black man can teach them how to be strong, yet still allow the Black man to be the head of the home. She can be taught how to love herself as a Black Queen, but also love, respect, and honor the Black man. Having a strong Black father present will allow daughters to see the strength, leadership, and importance of a Black man in her life, family, and community.

This is just a glimpse of why (regardless of how hurt we maybe), when children are involved a strong Black man needs to have contact and influence in their life. If not, many children will suffer from an unfulfilled void. This void is oftentimes captivated by many negative pressures. For instance, youth who do not have a positive male figure in their life resort to acting out behaviors. Many will say "*I did not have a father at home, therefore, I …*". The end of the statement may be, "*I did not care about life,*" "*I did what I wanted because my mother worked all the time,*" "*I had to be the man in my home because my father wasn't there,*" or, "*I looked to boyfriends to show me love, yet was used, although I thought I was experiencing love.*" When Black men are not active in a youth's life so many of the wrong doors have the potential of being opened. Let's go a step further. Many youth are being seduced by gangs who attempt to present a false image of a supportive big brother, father, or family. Such is often enticing when no strong Black father figure is present. Additionally, many children aspire to be the images depicted in the media. Those images are limited to entertainers and ignore our capabilities of being lawyers, CEOs, entrepreneurs, judges and doctors, positions which many Black men in the community serve. It is from these prevailing fields that mentors for our children need to be sought.

So sister, although you may be upset with the child's father, allow him to have contact and influence. Now if the father is not involved because of his own negligence or has passed away, find a male relative or friend who can fill that void. Failure to do so out of selfishness will result in perpetuating the pernicious fate of many of our youth.

Do You Know Her Experience?

What causes some Black women to judge another sister as "thinking she is all that" simply because that sister has reached levels of academic, career, or material success? While it is true that some successful Black women may align their internal worth with the dollar value of their material possessions, there are numbers of Black Accomplished Women (BAW) who maintain humility even in the midst of successes. The unfortunate truth is that a woman who is compelled to belittle the hard won success of her sister is driven by aborted self esteem and tragically deferred dreams.

The wounded woman's aborted self-esteem tells her that a BAW's rewards manifested out of the thin air of providence or inherited privilege. Her damaged psychological purview narrows to the present circumstance and blinds her to the realities of her sister's cause, effect, and consequence. It is from that perspective that she is able to deride a BAW as being all that when knowing nothing about the struggles and sacrifices along her sister's stony road to success. Unfortunately, the same faulty perspective that allows a wounded woman to demean a BAW's accomplishments also diminishes her own prospects for success by casting that success as unrelated and outside of her control.

So what happens to BAW in this peculiar chemistry of insecurity and internalized oppression? She stands isolated on the other side of an ever widening chasm of broken relationships and robbed of the essential benefits of the Black sisterhood. The tragic irony is that both, a BAW and her wounded sister, are being fed by the poisoning cord blood of the community's internalized oppression. Instead of being celebrated, a BAW is rejected. Instead of being supported, a BAW is ostracized. Instead of becoming a valuable resource for the community, a BAW becomes an overused target for its misdirected frustration. Tragically the very community that should receive the benefit of her experiential narrative turns its back. And what is the recourse? She may devalue accomplishments, aborting self-esteem in the vain hope of making those around feel less threatened. Alternatively, she may elect to mentally entomb within the cold comfort of her accomplishments. Ironically, by rejecting relationships with those who believed rejected her first, the myth is perpetuated by aloofness and supports the insecure claims of a wounded sister. An often occurred situation, but very few understand this illness behavior. It is not always that a BAW presents as if she is better than, she reflects and confronts the image of an unfinished and unfulfilled self when entering a room. As a result, the wounded sister could see the path she would have like to take. The wounded sister recognizes that life could have been different if she would have been more discerning with decision making. Additionally, some wounded sisters feel deficient because they come to acknowledge the absence of self-determination. This lack of self-determination results from the wounded sister embracing either society or someone in her immediate circle's limitations placed on her life, causing her to be cognitively immobilized for a season. However, it is not too late. There are numbers of BAW within the community to learn from. To reach her fullest potential, maybe it is time for the wounded sister to humble herself and pick the BAW's brain rather than ruminating on all the ways in which she failed to use hers. Everyone who became successful learned from someone else. Embrace a ~~BAW~~ around. They have experiences that can be built from to aid in accomplishing your goal set.

Understand, this symptomatic behavior from the illness of internalized oppression has impinged on the communal interactions and trickled into Black Sisterhood. We can learn and support one another in accomplishing both minor and major goals. However, first note the impact of this symptom and its maladaptive influence on sisterly interpersonal relationships. Such would aid the efforts of counteracting the adverse existing interactions within Black Sisterhood. The communities' existence is dependent on the strength of cohesive interdependent relationships among women. Accept the fact we exhibit these symptoms and humble ourselves in order to heal from the scars inflicted from these behaviors.

You Are a Queen?

Internalized oppression has infected Black women causing some to view their self worth solely based on physical attributes, minimizing intellectual capacity. The end result is many women define themselves based on their ability to attract or please a man sexually. Evidence of such is the embracing of revealing or tight styles of clothing to receive attention and a false representation of love. Additionally, there are those who internalize society's images of beauty, which portrays lighter skin tones, thin build and long straight hair as beautiful, resulting in the purchase of long hair weaves. These images are employed and adapted to make the world attracted to us. However, inside there is low self-worth and a minuscule outlook on life. As a result, we are not celebrated as Queens. Instead Black women are portrayed in films or other forms of media, produced by our oppressor as well as other Blacks, as women with limited cognitive ability whose greatest asset is physical thrill.

Contrary to the symptomatic behaviors that have become characteristic from years of struggle, we are Queens! We come from a people who are great. We come from individuals who were wealthy in finances and knowledge. We come from Kings and Queens who invented, organized governments and taught others about the sun, moon, and stars. We were made in the image of royalty, but often our present walk is that of a woman who does not know she is great.

Who is a Black Queen? A Queen does not allow others to define who she is or her potential. A Queen is a woman who nurtures, supports, and keeps family. She maintains a sense of spirituality to the Creator, the giver of life. A Queen works hard to accomplish aspirations, but does not belittle herself in the process. A Queen walks with head held high as she embraces life and destiny. A Queen also acknowledges and honors the ancestral greats. Black women, we are made in a Queen's image, unfortunately, some of us fail to exercise and demonstrate our Queen attributes.

Black women continue to demonstrate behaviors that present us as belittling to self, children, and community. These behaviors demystify our Queen status, having adopted the depreciating messages from enslavement as valid. As a result, there is a lack of self love and self knowledge. Although some may outwardly walk with heads high, internally heads are bowed low and backs are hunched under the rubble of crushed self-esteem. This mentally crippled state presents a false sense of self worth culminating with the abuse of our bodies, psyche, and family. We bring forth new life without a healthy sense of self, feeding children rotten emotional food through an under developed psychological umbilical cord. How do we raise Black children to love and respect themselves if we, who give life, do not respect and love ourselves? Some of us send an indirect message to our daughters that it is acceptable to be sexually promiscuous at an early age by the clothes we wear and the relationships we entertain. This causes them to look to the world for value and decreases their focus and ability to excel in academia which should be their primary concern. Some send messages to our sons that their value is measured by their demonstration of hardness, acts of aggression, violence, emotional disconnect, and coldness.

Letters to the Black Community

The very birth canals that once led to generations of collective greatness is currently birthing generations which engage in behaviors that serve to the collective's demise. What does it take for the Black Queen to rise up and resume their rightful place within the community? Let's redefine who we are. Let's work to reverse the negatives portrayed in society. It is going to take some time. However, start by looking in the mirror. Even though initially it might seem unbelievable, develop the habit of saying "I am a beautiful Black Queen". Spoken words become the belief system, which then lead to actions that impact our life, children, and community. Take some time to research the Kings and Queens of the collective's lineage. To understand our greatness, first understand the historical great persons we come from. We must make a commitment to set small and large goals regardless of what others say. Therefore, our children will witness the vitality of goal setting and determination, which they could emulate. Additionally, don't let age minimize goal setting and decision making. Oftentimes life experience aids in developing wisdom, which can be coupled with goals to birth an eminent experiential end. Furthermore, children loaned to the streets must be brought back home. It is the Black Queen's responsibility to aid in nurturing children to assure they reach their fullest potential regardless of whether the father is present; we must nurture and educate them. Therefore, society does not set the definition. But they are redefined by the positive individuals they can become.

The poisonous venom of racist mentalities have controlled and limited the potential to consummate the Queen's mark. It has also trickled into the veins of the children causing them to embrace life inconsequentially.

61

Regardless of life's obstacles and current stunt in growth, the final destination is predestined to be GREAT. Black women we are Queens, do not settle or position yourself to be anything less any longer.

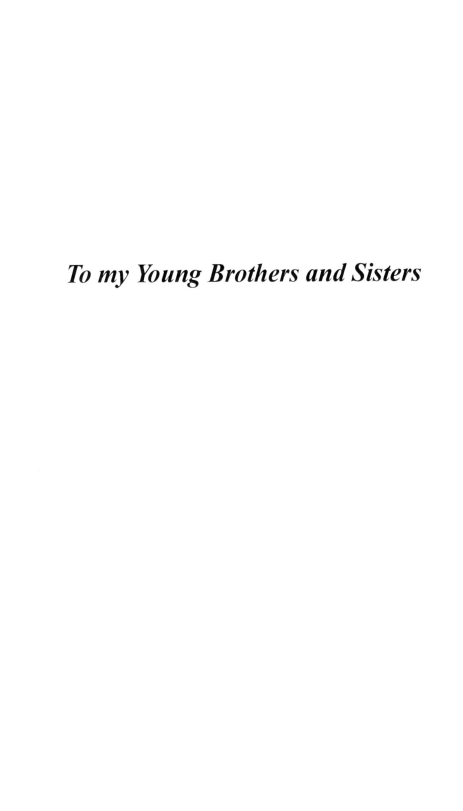

To my Young Brothers and Sisters

Preparation

It is fair to say a prepared mind is destined to accomplish its goal. According to Proverbs 21:5, *"the plans of the diligent lead surely to abundance, but everyone who is hasty comes only to poverty."* Thus, failure to thoroughly plan for the future results in an unfulfilled and malnourished life, invalidating a potentially rich destiny. From a psychological perspective, without direction or plan, we succumb to anything; including those persons and ideologies that could be detrimental resulting in a miniscule fate.

There remains a dilatable disparity between the college enrollment of Blacks and Caucasians. While racist systemic structures may bear a significant part of the blame for this disparity, we cannot ignore the self inflicted symptoms of the malady. Many lack knowledge of or drive to utilize resources to aid in our goal set. Some accept stereotypical factors that cause a minimizing of potential. Young brothers and sisters, too many of you own the belief that the pursuit of academic excellence equates to a betrayal of culture or more simply put, to acting White. Then to avoid ridicule and "stay Black", you sabotage opportunities for high academic achievement. On the other hand, those who do apply yourselves academically lack the impetus to seek out the information and resources required to prepare for your future.

Young brothers and sisters what are your aspirations? Do you want to travel, own a home, or have financial freedom? Then preparation starts now. Your journey will require a well thought out plan, measurable goals, and belief in self that your dreams can come true.

Begin to ask these next few questions:

1. What is my plan once receiving my High School Diploma?

2. Will I be ready to pursue my dreams—do I even have any worthwhile pursuing?

3. Will I be willing to endure hardship to accomplish my goals?

4. Will I be willing to go that extra mile to reach my goals?

Our history in America illustrates that we are a great people who can overcome adversity. So, brothers and sisters, whatever the challenge, there are no excuses for limited goal setting. Don't just get a job, establish a career. A career is a field of work that we engage for a life time, which has meaning, is rewarding, and offers stability. There is no reason why you cannot be the next generation of doctors, lawyers, owners of fortune 500 companies, politicians, and presidents. Brothers and sisters shake off the oppressor's message that your only option and value is the ability to run, bounce a ball, shake, sing, or dance. We owe the struggle of our ancestry much more.

Do not limit your future to aiming to be the next NBA/WNBA All-star player. Please note that according to the National Collegiate Athletic Association (NCAA), 3 in 10,000 high school males and 1 in 5,000 female seniors will be drafted (NCAA, 2011). Additionally, the NCAA reports that of the males who attend NCAA institutions, approximately, 1/75 (1.2 %) will be drafted in the NBA. Furthermore, with regard to females who attend NCAA institutions, less than 1 in 100 (.9%) will be drafted in the WNBA. Based on these reported statistics, it can be concluded that there are many great athletic talents, but very slim opportunities. Thus, broaden your aspirations and increase your opportunities to have a more predictable career. Why not learn the game during your tenure as a player, with the intent of managing or owning a team?

Move beyond societal limitations, and position yourself to accomplish enriched goals. Brothers and sisters believe that regardless of circumstances or challenges, you are of immeasurable value and possess an unlimited destiny. However, the ownership of that destiny, and the claiming of that value is your responsibility. Brothers and sisters, do not own the belief that you cannot go far in life because you may come from an inner city community which is labeled as producing only negativity. I am a prime example of what hard work, prayer, and dedication can do, regardless of where you are from. I am from what people call the ghetto, East New York, Brooklyn. But I did not let that stop me. I became a doctor at 29 due to long hours of preparing via studying and reading.

Understand that a passion can turn into a career that is both fulfilling and brings financial reward. For instance, if you enjoy animals why not pursue veterinary science and become a Vet. If you love children, why not study to become an elementary school teacher, a pediatrician, or a child psychologist. Attempt to volunteer in the area that you want to go to school and study. Go to the library and look up colleges or trade schools that offer your area of interest. Even if you are not clear about what the academic major may be, you can still research a college's offerings and admission requirements.

Practice writing about yourself as many will request a personal statement or an interview. However, in order to write a sterling letter and articulate clearly, you must develop and posses writing and vocabulary skills. You can start developing those skills by reading just for the sake of it.

Our enslaved ancestors lost their lives on the stony roads and underground railroads for educational freedom. During the Civil Rights movement, they braved canyons of bigotry and corridors of hate so that we could gain unrestricted access to education's liberty. You are reaping the fruits of the ancestors' labor and must go forth, exercising those rights as you stand on the shoulders of our ancestors' strength and the legacy they started.

Brothers and sisters whatever you set your mind and heart to do, PLAN to make and see it manifest. Nevertheless, before you can PLAN, you must have something to plan for. Ask, regardless of being accepted into a college or trade school, what career do I see myself doing? Take a few hours to think about this question; write down the answer if you have to. Once that is accomplished "**PLAN**"…

P--Prepare, Persistence, and Patience

Prepare- for potential obstacles that are or will be in your path of success that can cause you to fail, to get discouraged, or even quit.

Persistence- keep in mind that for anything good or worthwhile, there must be hard work. Position your psyche to work daily towards your goals. Do not give up when things become arduous.

Patience- know that success does not come overnight.

L--Lay and Learn

Lay- lay down a foundation. A High School diploma is the first step, now think about the future and map out the necessary steps needed to complete the dream.

Learn- learn new things daily even if it is a simple vocabulary word.

A--Analyze

Analyze- assess every situation whether it is positive or negative and use it as a learning experience. Also, analyze peers and surroundings. Keep yourself surrounded, at all times, with positive individuals and stay in enriching environments. Remember, being in the company of negative people or surroundings can serve as the demise of goals.

N--Never

Never- never give up; never say you can't. Most of the people in life who do not succeed are those who either don't try or those who gave up too easily or early.

Brothers and sisters, remember your destiny is unlimited. However, take responsibility to position yourself to actualize its fruits of wealth. Embrace your youth and future. Allow these words to be food for thought and power for preparation. Be the author of your destiny. Prepare yourself to accomplish immeasurable goals.

Brothers and Sisters, It's Preparation Time

Don't Forget to Turn Around

Growing up, many are encouraged to establish goals in order to have a meaningful future. Such normally entails completing high school and then either pursuing degrees, military ranks, trade school, or a good job. Nevertheless, many are not taught the significance of acquiring these achievements in order to assist those within the community, being in a position to give back and become persons of communal influence. Often times an indirect message is taught by commonly used statements indicating no community support for efforts. For instance, messages directly and indirectly communicated like 'why do you want a business' or 'why do you want to work in the community' indicates that after having made it, you should get as far away from the community as possible. However, the opposite should take place.

After you accomplish your goals, do not continue the generational divorce of the communal spirit of the ancestors. Use experiential wealth to help those within the community, particularly those who want help. On the journey to actualize your goals, you will obtain knowledge that other Blacks may not have the privilege to for various reasons. Do not stand in judgment, but turn around with the intent to assist another brother or sister in reaching to where you are. Remember your feelings on the journey? When there were very few people who looked like you serving as a person of contact, mentor, or advisor. Do not allow this impoverished cycle of unshared knowledge to continue. Regain that historical communal spirit and make our Black communities' problems your own.

Even if you do not want to live in a predominately Black community, aspire to be influential to the collective regardless of location. You may make it in society without the help of Blacks directly. Nevertheless, recall historically the ancestors fought hard for the civil liberties we now embrace. So regain and pass the communal torch. For it is by these efforts that we as a people will be able to rise up to our collective place and advance as a community.

I'm Proud of You

Brothers and Sisters, the world may attempt to allude to what you are not, but I know the reality of what you have the potential to become. Society may postulate what your future limitations are, but I know what you are predestined to be. Society tends to take the mishaps of a few and generalize it to the masses. However, I know there are many of you working hard to engage positive energy. Therefore, only greatness is birthed through you for the world to experience. So you may not have the greatest foundation or all the answers, but many of you do not let those constraints dictate and minimize an unlimited future. You continue to set goals and daily, work towards accomplishing them.

You do not allow excuses to become rationales that minimize potential, causing you to settle for what society says you can do. Some may say my father or mother was not there, we grew up poor, I struggled in school, or I had no friends. Although these are circumstances that may hinder growth potential, many embraced the resources that counteracted these voids and rose above what was lacking or needed to succeed. I am proud of you!

There are many that are interested in ..aving a bright future. Attending school regularly, attempting to maintain decent grades, and not seduced by the ignorant pressures from peers, some not only stand up for self, but stand out. You are different and choose not to be a follower of foolishness. You do not try and fit into a mold that is associated with acting out in which people watching would expect only a negative outcome. I am proud of you!

Many not only have goals, but priorities, understanding that there is a time and a place for all things, as now is the time for preparation of a great future. You understand that life will not be easy, but are willing to stay in the race and fight a good fight, accomplishing minor and major goals. People may be critical of your drive and determination because they cannot understand. Some may be envious of how you rise above each obstacle. Deep down inside, you acknowledge a destiny of greatness, therefore, you settle for nothing less. I am proud of you!

I know you are dating, but you do not allow romantic relationships or platonic friendships to become a distraction and hindrance to the aspired destination. It's not that you are anti-sociable, but knowing sometimes the need to be alone because the work to accomplish goals are not always a shared effort. You set a schedule and stick with it. Although others may complain and you can be flexible when time permits, there remain boundaries knowing you are on a mission to a great destination. I am proud of you!

Walking with your head high and back firm with pride, you are positioning yourself to rise above the obstacles. Like a boxer dodging the negatives that attempt to consume and convolute direction, you continue to soar on the journey. I am proud of you!

Young brothers and sisters, continue to walk on your journey knowing that there are persons cheering for your successes. Many of us believe in you. Although some may say you are a doomed generation, you are generation predestined for a future of greatness and influence. I am proud of you!

Thank you for being the future of predestined people bearing fruits of greatness... I am proud of you!

CONCLUSION

Understanding Our Greatness

The systemic structures of racism have caused the psyche of the Black community to develop a generational illness, internalized oppression. As discussed within the letters throughout this book, internalized oppression impacts our individual and collective worth, growth potential, and innate communal energies. It is hoped that the letters have raised awareness and sparked the motivation to execute positive changes within our communities.

Brothers and sisters, greatness is our truth. Although systemic structures attempt to keep us an oppressed people, generationally we triumph through the complications of this racist society. Some remain oblivious to the manifestations of racism and the resulting illness of internalized oppression. However, there remain many who are knowledgeable of this cyclical generational phenomenon and work to devise ways to navigate through it. Thus, as a people, we stay in an ever evolving position to keep breathing in a society that attempts to asphyxiate us to the point of annihilation.

Does the challenging experiences one has had weaken who they are, or does it aid in one's strength to overcome adversity? The vast experiences which have occurred within the lives of the collective are what give us strength and the ability to triumph. Within the Black community, life has been impacted by different 'ism(s)', including racism, classism, and sexism with the intent to mentally, physically, and economically cripple us for generations. The forcible plagues of slavery, illusions of just integration, and institutional racism have resulted in our illness of the mind. However, we continue to stride on this bigotry life journey with the medicinal energies of the ancestors. While we may not all work together, our history is a testament to our people's strength and determination.

Brothers and sisters, we are gifted. Some work to develop our gifts, while others do not nurture them. Some only exercise their talents for monetary gain and the approval of the majority class, while some choose to use it for the enrichment of the collective. Our unique talents are an asset to society; our unfortunate reality is that many are spoon fed the story of our alleged limited value. So ultimately, the question is not what we can do, but what will it take to realize our collective potential and move into our preordained place of leadership?

What happens when realizing we deliver greatness? We will begin to understand that there is the potential to negate the odds predicted against us. We will embrace the fact that our destiny is of unlimited wealth and no longer remain at the bottom of life's ladder. We would no longer be in the minority percentage in a vast number of positive outcomes in life, from degrees acquired to successful business owners. We will no longer stand in our own way. We will no longer belittle our brothers, sisters, children, and community. We will no longer allow society to dictate our lives, successes, worth, and destiny. When realizing our collective greatness, we will embrace it, use it to the collective's benefit, and soar on life's journey.

What happens when a Black man knows he delivers greatness? He would be void of doubt and neglect; but be determined and confident. He would set minor and major goals, determined to accomplish each, as he positions himself for his children and community to emulate his efforts. ~~He would resume his instinctual~~ place within the Black family and community as the head, having a stalwart voice. He would instill spiritual, ancestral, and communal energies within his family, setting and restoring the Black family unit.

What happens when a Black woman knows she delivers greatness? She will rely on the medicinal energies of the ancestors to aid in dismissing her role in perpetuating the illness of internalized oppression. She will speak words of healing into the Black man, youth, and community. It is by her words and prayers that our community births its mental, physical, and economical freedoms. She will align herself with the Black man as his greatest support, as they conquer the war of this systemic structure called racism.

What happens when Black youth realize they deliver greatness? They will accomplish any realistic goal, as they apply themselves, seek assistance when necessary, and remain determined. Our youth would no longer buy into the seductions of ignorance; including acting out behaviors to get them labeled, removed from school, or reduce their opportunities for economic growth.

What would happen if one day Black people woke up and realized they are destined to be greater than their current set of circumstances? What would happen if there was a realization that your life was destined to be fulfilled with wealth, health, liberation, and peace? When the Collective realizes that their life is predestined to be greater, the healing of this illness of internalized oppression would commence. We would work together to eliminate the symptoms, which will aid in increasing our mental, physical, and economic health. Thus, positioning all to no longer be the minority class, but resuming our enriched destiny of greatness and generational mental, physical, and economic wealth.

Brothers and sisters…greatness is our truth!

Glossary

1. Acting White - obtaining high academic achievement and/or employment status is considered a White only standard by some Blacks.

2. BABEL –confusion, turmoil

3. Caucasioned Diction – a slow drag of the words, attempting to make certain one sounds educated; some Blacks coin this as sounding White.

4. Counterfeit Elite Group - Blacks who have obtained wealth, education, house, car, etc. that feel they have arrived and/or are better than those Blacks who were less fortunate.

5. Discrimination - inequitable actions toward others based on race.

6. Ethnocentrism - to own and display pride in one's heritage, culture, and ancestry. To hold esteem to one's cultural experiences and a sense of belongingness to a collective.

7. Made It - ability to obtain material wealth, including car, house, education, money, and/or employment status.

8. Prejudice - assumptions about the abilities, motives, and intentions of others based on race.

Reference Page

1. Bowen-Reid, T. & Harrell, J. (2002). Racist Experiences and Health Outcomes: An Examination of Spirituality as a Buffer. Journal of Black Psychology, 28, 18-36.

2. Carr, J. & Kolluri, L. (2001). Predatory Lending: An Overview. Fannie Mae Foundation

3. NCAA Research (2011). Estimated Probability of Competing in Athletics Beyond the High School Interscholastic Level. NCAA Research updated September 27, 2011 from www.ncaa.org

4. Singleton, T., George, L., Dickstein, C., Thomas, H. (2006). Subprime & Predatory Lending in Rural America: Mortgage lending practices that can trap low-income rural people. University of New Hampshire, Carsey Institute, Policy Brief No. 4.

5. Williams, C. (2011). What Percentage of High School Players Make It to the NBA? Retrieved June 14, 2011 from www.livestrong.com , The Limitless Potential of You.

6. Williams, D., Neighbors, H., & Jackson, J. (2003). Racial/Ethnic Discrimination and Health: Findings from Community Studies. American Journal of Public Health, 93 (2), 200-208.